THE FREE MARKET
AND ITS ENEMY

The Free Market and Its Enemy

LEONARD E. READ

THE FOUNDATION FOR ECONOMIC EDUCATION, INC.

IRVINGTON-ON-HUDSON, NEW YORK   1965

THE AUTHOR AND PUBLISHER

Leonard E. Read, author of *Conscience of the Majority, Government—An Ideal Concept, Miracle of the Market, Students of Liberty, Why Not Try Freedom?, Elements of Libertarian Leadership, Anything That's Peaceful,* and other books and articles, is President of The Foundation for Economic Education, Inc., organized in 1946.

The Foundation is a nonpolitical, nonprofit educational institution. Its Senior Staff and numerous writers are students as well as teachers of the free market, private property, limited government rationale. Sample copies of the Foundation's monthly study journal, THE FREEMAN, are available on request.

PUBLISHED JULY 1965

Contents

se. The evil stems from energetic know-it-alls infesting society's agency for keeping the peace, this being their means of acquiring coercive power. Not knowing how little one knows detaches a man from reality. Psychosis! The result: creativities are turned against man's highest purpose.

The error of trying to make socialism work—or work better. The error of prophesying how a socialized activity would be conducted were it desocialized and left to the free market. The honesty and wisdom of confessing, "I don't know." Faith in the free market should rest on evidence from the miraculous demonstrations which abound on every hand.

The fear of chaos and the high price men will pay for order, or even the semblance of order. How chaos and order are mistaken one for the other. The chaos of the authoritarian society and the order of the free market society. Why the Moscow and Havana markets are chaotic and why market order prevails in Hong Kong. The free market economy is consonant with man's nature and destiny. Running away from life versus getting into it. The role of competition. The deception to avoid.

I think that I shall never see
A poem lovely as a tree.

A tree whose hungry mouth is prest
Against the sweet earth's flowing breast . . .

Poems are made by fools like me,
But only God can make a tree.

JOYCE KILMER

· 1 ·

The Drummer I Hear

My premise is that the destiny of man is to emerge or
evolve toward an advancing potential and that individual liberty is essential to such progress.

Unless a reader shares my premise, he will not respond to my reasoning; nor will it be possible for him
to arrive at my conclusions. He may have his eye set
on a star I do not see or, if seeing, care nothing whatsoever about. I side with Thoreau on this, ". . . perhaps
it is because he hears a different drummer. Let him
step to the music which he hears, however measured
or far away." If the music another hears be fame, or
fortune, or power, or ease and retirement, or longevity,
or anything less than individual emergence, I leave the
reconciliation to those with an itch for reform; it isn't,
as they say, my cup of tea.

The reflections which follow are not aimed at swerv-
ing anyone from whatever life purpose he may have set

1

for himself. That's his affair, not mine. Instead, these brevities are offered to those whose ideological and spiritual premise approximates my own: that man's earthly purpose is to expand one's own consciousness, as nearly as humanly possible, into a harmony with Infinite Consciousness or, in lay terms, to realize, as best one can, those creative potentialities uniquely his own. The lyrics to the music I hear have a clear refrain: the supreme purpose of life is "to hatch," to emerge, to evolve.

It seems hardly necessary to labor the point that liberty is an essential prerequisite to individual emergence. That ground is already well covered. Nor is it necessary, among serious students of liberty, to explain why economic freedom is a basic requirement. We are acutely aware that freedom of speech, of the press, of assembly, of religion—all of these—rise or fall as the market is freed or restricted. Our wishes cannot affect this truth; it has to be this way.

For anyone who accepts the above assumptions— all categorically expressed but easily demonstrable— it follows that his own evolving life depends on the fate of the free market. The market is not just a materialistic device, as many seem to believe. Spiritual expression is implicit in the free market, and the spiritual development of man is contorted by an interference with the market.

In view of its importance in man's evolution, the fact that freedom is declining in the market warrants our concern. Market freedom is declining partly because of our own meager understanding and poor explanation of it and, partly, because we incorrectly identify the free market's enemy.

These shortcomings in understanding and exposition stem (1) from letting a subtle and extremely important phase of the free market rationale escape our attention and (2) from identifying the enemy as government when, in fact, it is a widespread psychosis. My little treatise has no purpose other than to bring these overlooked points into focus.

But clear focusing requires a bit of background on the discoveries and explanations that have led to such development as the free market has had to date. I do not mean to underrate the many who have since refined their discoveries, but three distinguished thinkers stand out above the others:

Adam Smith for his development of the *specialization* thesis (1776);

Frederic Bastiat for the description of what he termed "an absolute principle": *freedom in transactions* (1840); and

Carl Menger for his discovery that the *value* of a good or service is determined *not objectively* by cost of production, *but subjectively* by what others will give in willing exchange (1870).[1]

---

[1] I have listed Smith, Bastiat, and Menger in the order of their appearance, not necessarily in the order of their importance.

One might conclude that anyone who understands specialization, freedom in transactions, and value—the underlying ideas which have spawned approximations of the free market—has everything in the way of economic understanding that a layman needs to know. But for the past century—and especially in our own daily news—there has been evidence aplenty that this knowledge, by itself, is inadequate. I shall argue that a key point in our rationale has been much neglected, if not missed entirely.

Concerning the Enemy

As to the enemy, it has never, to my knowledge, been brought clearly into focus but has been suspect for many decades. For instance, Herbert Spencer, writing in 1886, referred to it in *The Man Versus The State,* and Albert J. Nock wrote in somewhat the same vein, a half century later, in his volume, *Our Enemy, The State*.

My theme, *The Free Market and Its Enemy,* while generally consistent with what these writers had in mind, has little, if any, similarity in detail. Spencer's "Man" and Nock's "Our" are too generalized for anyone to grasp what it is I wish to explore: the miraculous workings of tiny creativities, the ultimate constituents of the free market, that institution on which depend all liberties, and thus man's emergence. And their "State" must have its perversions diagnosed if we are clearly to understand how it functions as the inhibitor and enemy of the free market. But I shall leave the enemy for a later chapter.

As to the free market: to reach correct conclusions it is necessary to employ appropriate categories in thinking. *Man*, as a category, is too complex to reveal how the free market works its miracles; indeed, the term *man* is as inappropriate for this analysis as are any of those broad, sweeping terms such as *society* or *civilization*. We must pick man apart, so to speak, and discover which of his numerous attributes relate to free market phenomena. Our task: to find that human attribute which appears to lie at the root of the matter, pose it as a hypothesis, and then test its validity in light of the evidence.

The human attribute which seems to me to have been overlooked or neglected in developing the rationale of the free market pertains to man's "creativities"—or the simpler term I prefer, his "think-of-thats."

Think-of-thats, by the way, is not of my invention; it is a term in common use by all of us whenever we hear of a novel thought or idea or activity. "Why didn't I think of that!" This is our natural reaction to creativity. And, appropriately, our response is always more of an exclamation than a question.

· 2 ·

*The Miraculous Market**

Awakening during the night, I flicked a bedside switch and soon the room was flooded with a Piano Concerto composed by Johannes Brahms. Perhaps the music itself induced a reflective mood: How explain this wonder of wonders for my enjoyment and with a near imperceptible effort on my part? What is at the root of this valued performance which comes to me "from out of the blue"?

Think of it! The finest orchestrations ever known to man, the most beautiful music any individual on earth has heard—all mine, and done for me privately when I want it, and where I want it, and for no more than the flick of a switch.[1] Staggering! Yet I, like most

---

* The substance of this chapter under the title, "The Miracles by Which We Live," was delivered as the Commencement Address, Interlochen Arts Academy, Interlochen, Michigan, on June 11, 1965.

[1] Admittedly, the connoisseur will not ascribe this quality to what he calls "tinned music."

Americans, take it for granted. We absorb the enjoyment and let it go at that; we drink of the cup without gratitude, as if the gift were automatically our due.

Mostly, we only revel in our blessings—if we do not overlook them entirely; rarely do we count them and seldom do we try to account for them. As to the musical miracle—one among millions—not only do we fail to reflect on how it comes about but, worse, we aren't even aware of having experienced a miracle. The sad fact is that if we do not recognize our countless gifts as blessings, particularly those which an attribute of man has had a part in shaping, such blessings are not long for this world.

What is it we have been glossing over in this instance of the music? For one thing, I—no magician—collapsed time and space. Imagine, an ordinary person being able to collapse time and space! Yet, a musical masterpiece, composed in the last century and some 3,000 miles from my home, was mine at my singular point in time and space! What, pray tell, would Aristotle, Peter, Paul, Caesar, Bacon, Lorenzo, Adam Smith, Bastiat, Menger, Brahms himself, or the late Andrew Dickson White have thought of that! No doubt about it, their answers could be lumped in a word, "Unbelievable!"

What's going on here? That's the question. To bring time into a comprehensible dimension, let us reduce the 50,000 years since Cro-Magnon man to one year. We observe that the first crude printing press came into existence a little more than four days ago. Machine-made paper, without which the printing press is insignificant for the mass of people, was a device of yesterday. Only in the last few hours has there been "sheet music." Thus, the storing or canning of music for the common man followed yesterday's sunrise. The same can be said for "tune language" or musical notations. Prior to these developments Joe Doakes and Richard Roe had nothing better than memory as a means of storing music.

No one knew how to make piano wire 3½ days ago. Tonal variations in wind instruments were achieved with the lips; valves are brand new. The first audible reproduction of recorded sound was an event that happened early this morning, and what we now call "fidelity" has been achieved during the last few minutes. And reflect on the "wireless" transmissions of recorded sound and its progressive development beginning this day and continuing to the present moment.

I have, in the above, mentioned only suggestive milestones—a few among thousands—that, taken together, have made a magician of me in an area where I know next to nothing: by the mere flick of a switch I collapsed time and space, permitting a private audience with the finest music known to man.

Bear in mind that this magic is but an isolated instance among countless others. For example, I am writing this copy on an electric typewriter. The antecedents of this phenomenon defy one's imagination, going back, as they do, to the Paleozoic period and the decomposition of vegetable matter, and the formation of coal: works of nature. Then the works of man: mining the coal for fuel and steam, the making of engines and dynamos and transmission lines. Take this mechanical marvel itself: Nature and man working together, converting decayed vegetation of millions of years ago into a writing machine for my use! What fantastic creativity at work! What a remarkable conversion of potential energy into flowing, useful, kinetic energy!

For the most part we make no effort to account for these miracles by which we live or, if we do, we settle for some oversimplified answers which must, perforce, fall far short of accuracy.[2] We conclude, for instance, that Johann Gutenberg invented the printing press, James Watt the steam engine, Robert Fulton the steamboat, Guglielmo Marconi the wireless, Alexander Graham Bell the telephone, Thomas Alva Edison the phonograph, and so on. We have a slipshod tendency to personalize phenomena as did the ancients who ascribed the quality of gods to forces that baffled them

---

[2] Considerable criticism is directed at my insistence on the use of the term "miracle." The critics, while agreeing that there is much which presently transcends human knowledge, will not allow that there is anything in the whole Cosmic Scheme but what can, sooner or later, be understood, scientifically verified, and explained. I shall let them have their way. As for me, I have discovered that the more I know, the more do I become exposed to the unknown and what I believe to be *the unknowable*. I see elements of the miraculous in everything.

and gave names to the gods they contrived. Like them, we look for heroes and name them inventors. But this explains little or nothing. And, no doubt, these individuals thought of themselves as the creators of the artifacts linked with their names. Most of us find little difficulty in taking more credit for originality than the facts warrant.

Who Invented the Jet?

I must not, in this attempt to develop my central point, rob Edison and these other very remarkable men of their glory. But it is of vital importance that we know precisely their real claim to fame.

Consider, by way of analysis, the largest manufacturer of commercial jets. That company employs several thousand engineers. It is safe to say that not a waking hour passes, in any day of any year, without some of these engineers experiencing several little creativities, tiny think-of-thats, discoveries, ideas for the improvement of an already amazing artifact, a veritable magic carpet. True, an engineer, now and then, will have a whole series of think-of-thats, amounting to a breakthrough; many others have such experiences less frequently, and probably not a one of them draws a complete blank. The variation factor may be as great as 1:1000—or even greater.

Search out the engineer who today experiences more creative ideas for improvement of the jet airliner than any of the others. Can it be said that he invented the jet? The notion that such a person invented the jet is just as absurd as crediting any of his predecessors with the achievement. This individual has only added his own think-of-thats to literally trillions of antecedent creativities, and no more can be claimed for any who came before him: Charles Goodyear who, in 1839, added some discoveries that led to the hot vulcanization of rubber; Orville and Wilbur Wright had some relevant creativities. And what about the thousands who had ideas leading to wind tunnels? Or the countless persons who thought how to alloy metals for strength, lightness, and heat resistance? Or the aerodynamicists whose creativities resulted in the sweptwing? And what about those individuals who discovered that treating paper with a mixture of ferricyanide and ammonium ferric citrate would give us blueprint paper?[3] And the teachers who taught the engineers? Or what could have been accomplished had an alphabet not been contrived, or zero conceived?[4] Employing this line of reasoning, the modern jet is but a singular culmination of creativities that can be traced back to

---

[3] Blueprints important? It took 52 sets of 22,000 separate, original drawings for a recent new model jet!

[4] Zero, conceived during the early Middle Ages, "was the crowning achievement in the development of a number system in which calculation with large numbers was feasible. Without it modern astronomy, physics, and chemistry would be impossible." Without the conception of zero, the modern jet would be inconceivable. See *Columbia Encyclopedia.*

the think-of-thats which harnessed fire, and which accounted for the first wheel and a crude stone ax.

The remarkable thing about Edison and his perceptive kind is the profusion of creativities which flows through their fertile minds. But they—every one of them—only add their own think-of-thats to millions of antecedent think-of-thats. What they do, as contrasted with most of us, is to supplement the antecedent build-up with precisely the right creativities which, when added, bring the new total to a patentable, usable, practical, marketable status. Theirs are *crowning* achievements—this is their genius.

Did Edison, by adding think-of-thats which finished off or completed the phonograph, for instance, make a greater contribution to that artifact than his predecessors? It seems to us that he did. Yet, we aren't really competent to allocate credit. What are we to say about the ones who first thought of how to harness fire, and the others, without whom Edison's accomplishment would have been impossible? How few would be the think-of-thats among us today, if antecedent creativities had developed nothing more than the harnessing of fire! We would experience little more in the way of creativities than dumb beasts. But into this barren situation let us imagine that a jinni has tossed us some sheets of tin and a pair of tin snippers, both the tin and the snippers being culminations of millions of creativities. How such an act would stimulate think-of-thats! In short, the greater the number of antecedent creativities at one's disposal, the easier is his creativity. It is, therefore, quite possible that the greatest credit should go to those who accomplished breakthroughs when the antecedent creativities were fewer than at any given present, and creativity, thus, more difficult.

The above reflections on crowning achievements are meant only to dispel our tendency to oversimplification and to center attention where it belongs: *on trillions upon trillions of tiny but complex and interacting creativities, the free flowing of which is, in fact, the free market!* Think of our gifts, these artifacts by which we live, not only as the discoveries of identifiable geniuses but as the outcroppings of a flowing, growing, evolving energy that goes back to the beginning of human consciousness. The miraculousness of the free market can be appreciated only when this concept is grasped, only when it is conceived of as flowing energy *in depth*.

These creativities, flowing through the minds of countless human beings over the ages, are the ultimate constituents of the artifacts by which we live, bearing a striking likeness, in their behavior, to the ultimate constituents in nature: molecules and atoms.[5] Just as atom-composed molecules, by some inexplicable proc-

---

[5] I use the term "ultimate" with tongue in cheek. Who am I to say that the atom is the ultimate constituent in nature? Atomic scholars, after telling all they know, ask: "Does each proton and neutron in the nucleus [of the atom] have a dense core with a hazy, cloudlike thinning around it? Can it be that they have structure? Do protons and neutrons contain even more fundamental particles?" See *The Atom* by George L. Bush and Anthony A. Silvidi (New York: Barnes and Noble, Inc., 1961), p. 139.

ess, miraculously configurate to form a blade of grass
or a tree or whatever, so do creativities, as they manifest themselves through the minds of men, strangely
configurate to form the goods and services which, before we discover their utility, only amaze and intrigue
us.[6]

Strangely configurate! Indeed, how can we account
for creativities flowing through millions of persons,
very few of whom ever know of each other, combining
to form these things we find useful? Unless we realize
that we with our own individual contributions only
partially account for these phenomena, we shall never
fully grasp the miracle of the free market. On earlier
occasions I have erroneously written that these creativities merge or configurate into useful artifacts as a response to human demand and necessity. But, clearly,
there was no demand—on the surface of life, at any
rate—for Brahms' masterpieces before they existed.
Only after they came into being did the demand develop. Who demanded electric power and light before
anyone ever heard of such energy? Fire was not demanded prior to the think-of-thats and discoveries that
harnessed it; until then, fire was an awesome, fearful
force. How, then, are we to explain these flashes of
brilliance which the recognized needs of man do not

---

[6] It is after we adopt an artifact and begin to think of it as a
necessity that we no longer marvel at the wonder of it. Familiarity
makes it commonplace; we lapse into a supercilious indifference,
and tend to stand in awe of nothing but novelty.

induce? *These creativities proceed from a Source exterior to man!*

Further, it becomes clear that *these creativities pace our demands and define our necessities.* The demand develops after these artifacts are formed by the creativities, and if the demand be great enough, the artifacts may well become necessities, a necessity being anything on which we become dependent. To illustrate: A hundred years ago there was no demand for electric power and light. Today the demand is enormous. And what's more, we have become dependent on this form of energy; were it suddenly eliminated, millions of us would perish; it is, indeed, a necessity.

Our Lives Depend on Trade

Assuming the above observations to be reasonably accurate, the free market takes on a new and even startling significance. To an extent rarely appreciated, creativities and their uninhibited exchanges—the free market—decide our demands and necessities; they "lead us by the nose," as the saying goes. But, is this so strange, and is it at odds with proper human aspirations? Not if it be conceded that the creativities flowing through the minds of men proceed from the same Creation that is responsible for the Cosmos and Nature. I can see not an iota of evidence to the contrary.

Nature, be it observed, "leads us by the nose." That is, oceans, lakes, forests, climates, deposits, soils, the sun's energy have powerful influences on where and how long we live, what our occupations are, what and with whom we exchange. Do not the flora and fauna have much to do with our individual destinies? Creation, as we observe it in Nature, is the fact given; it is the preordained arena of the human situation; it is the framework within which we better or worsen ourselves; choices about the over-all framework are not ours to exercise.

I am affirming that creativities, as we observe them flowing through the minds of men, have the same Source as the creations we observe in Nature. Creative phenomena, once they take place, are as much the fact given as neutrons, protons, atoms, molecules, Old Sol. Man's creativities, discoveries, think-of-thats also control human destiny, the road we shall travel, where and how long we shall live, what and with whom we shall exchange, and so on.

If these creativities and their free flowing—the free market—do in fact have an overpowering influence in charting human destiny, is the fact to be deplored or rejoiced in? The answer must depend on at least two considerations.

The first has to do with the individual's major premise. If one's earthly goal is a freezing of the status quo, or getting out of life as distinguished from getting into a more intense quality of life, or avoiding the pain of change, growth, stretching the faculties, then, for certain, logic dictates that the fact be deplored.

But one can exult in the fact if his earthly goal be an expansion of consciousness, as nearly as possible, into a harmony with Infinite Consciousness (Creation or God). Taking the ever-changing, always-unexplored road which new creativities lay out before us is compatible with evolution and consistent with the realization of one's own creative potentialities.

The second consideration has to do with the nature of the creativities themselves. Man has the choice of going wrong as well as right—and not all think-of-thats are on the side of the angels. Destructive or contorted ones take us on a road that leads to disaster, and these are to be deplored; only the constructive ones are to be looked upon favorably. I believe it is possible to identify the forces which promote the constructive ones as well as the forces which stimulate the destructive ones. But this must wait until we come to the discussion of the free market's enemy.

The Spiritual Nature of the Market

In concluding this chapter, I re-emphasize that my only object is to gain a better insight into the miracle of the free market. Unfortunately, many persons who are capable of improved insights regard the free market as crass and materialistic and, thus, unworthy of their thoughtful attention.

On the contrary, I contend that there is no higher cultural pursuit—be it music, art, poetry, drama, or whatever—than acquiring an appreciation of the mysteries of the free market. This phenomenon, I believe, is a reflection of spiritual forces at work. At least this radical contention deserves a hard look.

The artifacts by which we live—from the wheel to an electronic computer—are generally thought of as having only materialistic properties. But what are they, really? This much we know: they are brought into existence by applying human creativities to the resources of Nature. We need only ask ourselves, what are creativities? And what are resources?

Creativities, ideas, think-of-thats, discoveries are as spiritual as the spirit of inquiry. Try, for instance, to find any materialistic substance in a thought. Ideas are spiritual or intellectual energy, as free of materialistic properties as is a dream.

What of the natural resources: coal, water, ore, trees? Of what are these constituted? Like human beings, they are structured of atoms, 30 trillions of which could be placed on the little period at the end of this sentence, without overlapping. And what is an atom? It is energy, as void of substance as a whisper from space, or light, or a radio wave, or a thought.[7]

---

[7] The term "materialistic," when ascribed to artifacts, derives from a lack of depth perception. It has application to a table, for instance, only when no more can be perceived than a table with "substantial" properties. "Materialistic" loses its meaning, that is, it becomes nonapplicable when a table is perceived as energy in motion. See "Introduction," *The Nature of the Physical World* by Sir Arthur Stanley Eddington (New York: The Macmillan Company, 1928).

In the final analysis, everything we conceive or perceive is radiant energy proceeding from Creation. It more than resembles, for it is, in fact, a spiritual force. Radiant energy configurates in ways beyond calculation. There isn't a quality we attribute to anything— dull, bright, red, blue, solid, liquid, dead, alive, noisy, conscious, intelligent—but what is radiant energy in some of its infinite manifestations.

The musician, artist, poet, dramatist combine energy in the form of creativities with energy in the form of artifacts, and the combination of energies shows forth in new energy configurations such as Brahms' *Piano Concerto in D Minor,* Goethe's *Faust,* Leonardo da Vinci's *The Last Supper*, Shakespeare's *King Lear*.

Achieving an understanding of free market phenomena is but gaining an awareness—a radiant energy manifestation itself—as to what makes possible such things as music, poems, paintings, plays, jet planes, or whatever. It is the study of free-flowing spiritual forces and the effect on them of man-made obstructions and contortions. It is learning about man's part in Creation. It is a cultural process in itself and fundamental to all else that is cultural.

Reflect, again, on what takes place when the beautiful music of a bygone master is yours for the mere flick of a switch. What is the nature of the miracle you so easily perform? It is this: trillions upon trillions of human creativities, extending back to the think-of-thats which harnessed fire, and all of the relevant discoveries since that prehistoric event, are automatically ushered to your service. No writer of magic ever thought to give his jinni such a power as the free market bestows on you and me!

But we must not be led astray by dwelling unduly on the musical miracle. We also should be aware that the very same phenomena are at work when the grocer exchanges a can of beans for thirty cents, or when we drink a cup of coffee, or when we press a button and let the free market wash dishes while we read a book.

It isn't easy to understand how the free market washes dishes and performs countless other services in view of the fact that man has contended against creativities and their exchanges over the centuries—as if these were his foe. The market has never been, nor is it now, freed from stupidities and man-made hindrances. In the face of such frustrations, how can we explain the countless creative achievements?

Had all the little think-of-thats and their exchanges been completely thwarted, mankind would never have advanced beyond Cro-Magnon status. That the human situation has shown some improvement stems from the fact that stupidities and hindrances have rarely been able wholly to contain and suppress these creative energies; authoritarian arrangements have seldom succeeded in insulating them. These creative energies are everlastingly leaking through the porosity of destructive customs, taboos, edicts, laws. Manifestation is their destiny, and their power to escape constriction resembles lightning as it picks its way along lines of least resistance. Block it here and it goes there. "Thy will be done!"

The power of creative energies to manifest themselves in the face of man-made obstacles accounts for the progress we observe even when the worst elements in society get on top.[8] But these worst people and their numerous inanities, by themselves, are incapable of putting a crimp in evolution. The danger is that millions of people, observing progress and human intervention proceeding simultaneously, are tempted to correlate the two and, thus, regard the foolish actions as the cause of the progress. They may fail to see that the progress is *in spite of* the obstruction. In such situations the destructive forces become so overpowering that whole civilizations decline and fall. Historically speaking, the setbacks are temporary, but who wants to be an accomplice to evolutionary setbacks?

To avoid such disaster, we must know the nature of the evil forces.

---

[8] Lord Macaulay, beginning his *The History of England* in 1839, while not assigning reasons identical to mine, observed progress and destructive forces going on at the same time: "In every experimental science there is a tendency towards perfection. In every human being there is a wish to ameliorate his own condition. These two principles have often sufficed, even when counteracted by great public calamities and by bad institutions, to carry civilisation rapidly forward. . . . It has often been found that profuse expenditures, heavy taxation, absurd commercial restrictions, corrupt tribunals, disastrous wars, seditions, persecutions, conflagrations, inundation, have not been able to destroy capital so fast as the exertions of private citizens have been able to create it." See his Chapter III.

· 3 ·

The Enemy: A Psychosis

When we flick a switch and flood the room with music, or drink a cup of coffee, or read a book, or press a button to wash the dishes, or ride a jet, we are witnessing not *things* but *performances* that have their beginnings as far back as the advent of human consciousness.[1] The appropriate question in each instance is not "What is this?" but, rather, "What's going on here?"

What's going on here? That's the question. Of course, from the very beginning, a few of man's actions have been in his own interest. Had this not been true the human species would long since have been extinct. But progress has always been stubborn. Over the millennia, man seldom has seen clearly which of his economic actions made for progress and which for regress. It has been hit or miss, as we say.

---

[1] An enlightening explanation of the performance concept is "You Cannot Pick a Dandelion" by Arthur P. Moor, *The Freeman*, April, 1964.

For instance, there is evidence that robbery was the first labor-saving device, and history is replete with looting and the devastation of neighboring peoples as a means of gaining wealth. Such people simply were not good economists. And billions of individuals, if they had any moral scruples at all, embraced them only formally; they were unable to give economic adaptation to their moral inclinations. Even to this day, men give lip service to the Ten Commandments and the Golden Rule as they pray to God for victories in their numerous slaughters, thefts, and injustices.

Now and then societies have emerged from barbarism but, perhaps, more fortuitously than rationally— societal accidents! A civilization appears, its members revel in its glory, and the civilization declines and falls. And the end of these fluctuations is not yet.[2]

Again, we ask, "What goes on here?" We should keep in mind that the slow economic progress prior to the beginning of the nineteenth century was for lack of ability to distinguish between sound and unsound economic actions. As stated above, some actions must have been sound or man would not have survived. But what were those sound actions?

_____

[2] These fluctuations appear to be a part of the evolutionary process. Man gains some wisdom and prospers and, as a result, thinks he has "made it." But there is more wisdom to be gained—always more—if he is to emerge. Unless man reaches the point where he can rationally will his own growth, the historical tumbles serve only to wake him up again. Evolution and devolution follow on each other's heels with rhythmic regularity, with evolution gaining over the millennia.

Eventually, light began to dawn—light in the form of discerning observations. Adam Smith observed that when men specialized, as distinguished from each doing everything for himself, productivity greatly increased. Smith, however, did not invent specialization. He merely took note of what had been overlooked; he saw that certain human practices were efficacious and he went on to develop the explanation that made the fact understandable.

Of course, specialization, by itself, is fatal. If one specializes only in clothing and another only in food—without exchange—the former will starve while the latter freezes. Specialization, to assure economic progress, depends upon exchange. But exchange at whose discretion? A political authority's? It was Bastiat and others, several decades after Smith's great work, who observed and explained *freedom in transactions*. Two steps in the rationale of the free market had been made by 1850.

The Determination of Value

There remained, however, a missing link in the rationale: the determination of value. How can economic justice be served if there is no valid basis for deciding the value of a good or service? Is value to be set by the amount of effort exerted? No, replied Carl Menger and others (1870) to this labor theory of value; the value of a good or service is what others will give for it in willing exchange. Again, these men did not invent the marginal utility theory of value; they discovered it by observing man's actions. Wrote its greatest theoretician, Eugen von Böhm-Bawerk:

For centuries, long before science set up the doctrine of marginal utility, the common man was accustomed to seek things and abandon things . . . he practiced the doctrine . . . before economic theory discovered it.[3]

The rationale of the free market has become known only to those of the most recent generations, and with the rationale has come a considerable practice. The result? A veritable outburst of productivity! We now can make clothing from sand, metal from sea water. We can run factories and light our homes and wash our dishes by releasing the power of the atom. We can deliver the human voice around this earth in one-seventh of a second, human beings from Los Angeles to New York in four hours, a symphonic production into everyone's home in motion and color at the time of performance. We can put TV sets on the moon. We can make observations two billion light years into space. There isn't a desirable artifact but what we can produce in profusion.

But note carefully that it is "we" who can do all of these things. "I" cannot do a single one of them. No individual can make a jet, or an automobile, or a dish-

---

[3] See *Capital and Interest*, Vol. II, by Eugen von Böhm-Bawerk (South Holland, Ill.: Libertarian Press, 1959), pp. 203-204.

washer, or a book, or even a wooden lead pencil. "I," in the absence of "we," am hopelessly helpless, not being able to raise the food "I" eat, build the home in which "I" live, make the clothes "I" wear, produce the music "I" enjoy. "I" am abysmally ignorant of what "we" have brought into existence, being only partially knowledgeable in a tiny area of specialization.

While specialization, freedom in transactions, and the correct concept of value have paved the way for an undreamed of affluence, this achievement has brought with it a new and destructive confusion, one that threatens to undo all the good work: the belief that "I" am the creator of the gifts which "we," over the centuries, in collaboration with Creation, have bestowed. "I," in ever so many instances, have become a know-it-all! As proof of this, merely observe the numerous members of our society who can gratify every wish in goods and services—many of whom do nothing at all—people, who less than a few generations ago would have been living in poverty, and note how unaware they are of what brought on their affluence. All too often their attitude is, "See what 'I' have done!"

A Warning about "We"

May I hasten to add a word of caution. "We" is a noncommunicative and misleading word in this instance, for it suggests collective as distinguished from individualistic action. Nothing could be further from the truth. What "we" can now do is only what is made possible by countless creativities, ideas, discoveries, think-of-thats freely exchanging and interacting over the millennia. Because these ideas do come from or flow through the minds of men, there is a tendency to personify the performance and, thus, the use of "we." "We," in this context, is simply the free market, nothing else.

Nonetheless, the achievements of this free market are arrogated to an "I" in dangerous proportions. This is a false and an unwarranted egotism. It is an estimation of self so remote from reality that it must be described as a psychosis. There would be no occasion for concern if only a few persons were to think of themselves as Napoleon; but, when millions of people are the victims of this complex, take heed!

The real enemy of the free market is this very know-it-all-ness![4]

Contrary to what many antisocialists claim, the enemy of the free market is not the state, that is, if "state" be used interchangeably with government. This formal agency of society, when organized to keep the peace, to invoke a common justice under law, and to inhibit and

---

[4] " . . . our limitation is something that can only be experienced and laid hold of by actually living. And the knowledge of our limitation is not a certain knowledge that can be preserved in a proposition, but rather is a thoroughly uncertain knowledge against which we constantly rebel, which we constantly ignore, and dismiss from our minds." From *Existence and Faith* by Rudolph Bultmann (Meridian, N. Y., 1960), p. 63.

penalize fraud, violence, misrepresentation, and predation is a necessary and soundly principled ally of the
free market.[5] When we mistakenly identify an institutional ally as a foe and cast our barbs at it, we act
against ourselves, and downgrade our philosophy. By
so doing, we become our own enemy.

To settle and exclusively dwell on overextended government as the enemy is to let the real culprit go un-
noticed or, to employ a metaphor, it is to concentrate
on smoke abatement while the house is burning down.
But let's start from the beginning and see if we can
shed some light on how we mistake effect for cause or,
more precisely, why we blame distorted government
while giving no attention to the psychosis which is responsible for the distortion.

So Much Is Missed

Nothing is more common to mankind than ignorance. Lecomte du Noüy, the noted French scientist,
points out that man's image of his universe rests on
reactions determined in him by less than one-trillionth
of the vibrations which surround him—that less than
one vibration in a trillion leaves any trace in his consciousness.[6] This is a sobering observation and lends

---

[5] I have tried to spell out and explain the principled role of
government in *Government—An Ideal Concept*. (Irvington-on-
Hudson, New York: Foundation for Economic Education, 1954).

[6] See *Human Destiny* by Lecomte du Noüy. (Mentor, 1963).

credence to the idea that just plain ignorance is our lot. By nature, man is fallible. Never being able to know much, regardless of how much knowledge is acquired, is a built-in condition of the human species. Escaping from ignorance, that is, progressing everlastingly into a state of consciousness, is an eternal process, and there is no end to eternity. To grow in harmony with Infinite Consciousness is a goal toward which man can ever strive but never attain. Any individual, aware of this natural ignorance, will readily realize that the more he knows, the more he will expose himself to the unknown. As he knows more, the more conscious will he be of how little he knows. But by knowing something, however little, man does ascend and improve his situation; in fact, he comes, in an infinitesimal way, to share in Creation. Viewed broadly enough, this appears to be human destiny. In any event, moving from the depths of ignorance to lesser ignorance is a process favorable, not antagonistic, to the unobstructed flow of creativities: the free market.

I repeat, ignorance, of itself, is not the enemy of the free market. Ignorance is universal among men! Were sheer ignorance the culprit, there never would have been any freedom in the market, none whatsoever. The real foe is the *ignorance of being ignorant;* it is the ignorance of the fact that man in his earthly station is limited at best to a growth in knowledge. Any person not in this state of awareness is, perforce, a know-it-all. Keep the eye peeled for know-it-alls, because they are authoritarian in spirit. The explanation? Any person unaware of a Creation over and beyond his own mind obviously cannot but believe in his own omniscience. This is self-evident. Does it not follow, then, that such an individual has no means of envisioning an improved human situation except as other persons are made to reflect his own imperfect self?

Fortunately, most know-it-alls are not influential because they are not energetic; they are comparative do-nothings. Ever so many on either side of the ideological fence fall into this category; at most, they are only followers. Like the fly on the chariot wheel—believing it was he who was kicking up all the dust—these folks naïvely believe the affluence in which they find themselves to be of their own doing. Having everything "figured out," they do no serious reading, writing, thinking, exploration and, thus, are ideologically sterile. Their initiative and energy together are exhausted from seeking opponents to inveigh against, or friendly Georges to worship, vote for, or let do. Personally irritating as they may be, these people no more alter the situation in which humanity finds itself than does the idle, vacuous chit-chat heard at cocktail parties.

The Energetic Ones

When trying to find persons who shape the course of events—for better or worse—look for the energetic ones. Not the physical jumping jacks but, rather, those individuals with active minds and restless, determined spirits. So far as man has any control of his destiny, it is only these energetic persons who account for the swerves in the road we travel; they are always in the vanguard leading toward evolution or devolution; they are humanity's constructive or destructive agents.

These energetic individuals fall into two broad categories. First, on the constructive side, there are those who succeed in turning their energy inwardly to their own development, emergence, growth. When this happens, the best in each is brought out; and from this number come the historical oversouls and enlightenment. Reflect on Jesus of Nazareth. Other givers of light come to mind: Hammurabi, Ikhnaton, Ashoka, Guatama Buddha, Lao-tse, Confucius, Moses, Socrates and, closer to our own time, Beethoven, Milton, Leonardo da Vinci, Goethe, Rembrandt, Edison, Pasteur, Henri Poincare—and, unquestionably, there are many presently in our midst.

Second, on the destructive side, are the energetic know-it-alls. Know-it-all-ness allows no room for improvement; thus, these psychotics make no effort to turn their unusual drive inwardly; they produce no light. Ignorant of their ignorance, it is their ignorance which they must inflict on the rest of us if they can find the means to do so. But there is no way for them to realize their ambition without employing compulsion. The know-it-alls, by themselves, do not possess enough compulsive force to inflict their ignorance on the rest of us. What to do? They seek and often obtain positions in society's agency of organized force: government. In short, they get themselves a constabulary. We obey their edicts, or we take the consequences. In these circumstances, mankind is damned by a Genghis Khan, Napoleon, Hitler, Stalin, and the like. One has no difficulty in finding examples of energetic know-it-alls—small fry and giants—in either the past or present. They are all about us.

Individuals Make Government Grow

Government, per se, is not the enemy of the free market; it is not the root of the authoritarianism that is plaguing us. Rather, it is the psychotics—the little Napoleons—who have taken roost in government. We do not condemn education as an institutional ideal because of an influx of faulty teachers. No one suggests abandoning religion when inferior persons infiltrate the clergy. Nor should we downgrade society's agency for keeping the peace because unpeaceful know-it-alls have taken over. Government, per se, is not our problem. Instead, we have a widespread, pervasive psychosis on our hands; only rarely is there an individual who is completely free of it.

The discipline that deals with a psychosis is psychiatry. Does this mean that the free market devotee must attain skills as a psychiatrist as well as a political economist? Isn't it adequate first to master and then to extend and refine the works of Adam Smith, Bastiat, Menger, Mises, and their brilliant kind? Must the devotee of liberty also develop an understanding of the human psyche? Travel the road of Carl Jung?[7] For all I know, this may be among the new requirements in human evolution; there is evidence that it is. But, at the very least, we must be able to identify and have some understanding of the psychosis here in question —in ourselves as well as in others—lest it spell our undoing.

This psychosis is a detachment from reality. It is a self-assessment that has no basis in fact. I refer to the victims as "little Napoleons" because Napoleon was the perfect archetype. For example, his domestic affairs were a mess, and his numerous family drove him to distraction. While he couldn't run the affairs of his home life, he entertained no doubt about his ability to manage the world. Herbert Spencer described this kind of mentality in this way:

. . . home experiences daily supply proofs that the conduct of human beings baulks calculation. He has given up the thought of managing his wife and lets her manage him. Children on whom he has tried now reprimand, now punishment, now suasion, now reward, do not respond satisfactorily to any method; and no expostulation prevents their mother from treating them in ways he thinks mischievous. So, too, his dealing with his servants. . . . Yet, difficult as he finds it to deal with humanity in detail, he is confident of his ability to deal with embodied humanity.

---

[7] See *The Undiscovered Self* by Carl Jung. (Mentor, 1959).

Citizens . . . the great mass of whom belong to classes having habits and modes of thought of which he has but dim notions, he feels sure will act in certain ways he foresees, and fulfill ends he wishes.[8]

Bear in mind that Hitler was only an indifferent paper hanger; he was competent at nothing except leading millions to believe that the world would be better off were he in charge. Stalin, another victim of the same psychosis, tried first theology and then train robbery before he elected to manage mankind.

Signs of the Illness

But if we laymen are to take the first step in psychiatric diagnostics, we will recognize that a person does not have to make the enormous leap from personal failure to delusions of world-wide grandeur to suffer this psychosis. These delusions come in fragments of varying dimensions. Whenever any individual loses account of how little he knows and believes that his guidance might supplant that of the free market to universal advantage, even though the sector in which he would intervene be minor, he has contracted this mental illness. Nor does an ignorance of his limitations or of the phenomena he would molest alter his case. A psychosomatic illness is an illness whether or not its causes are known.

---

[8] See *The Man Versus The State* by Herbert Spencer (Caldwell, Idaho: Caxton Printers, 1940).

To laugh at persons who think they are Napoleon is, in most instances, to laugh in one's own face. And to enumerate the specific instances in which the American people, today, play the role of little Napoleons, not only innocently but with a sense of righteousness, is to laugh in almost everyone's face, so far down the Napoleonic road have we gone. To be specific is to flaunt the mores—all over the place! Hardly a person but who would be offended were the whole tiresome list of interventions examined—from minimum wage laws to paying farmers not to farm, you name it![9]

Consumers May Be Trusted

I asserted in a previous chapter that not all creativities are on the side of the angels, that they can be destructive as well as constructive, and that the determining forces can be identified.

Creativities will tend to be constructive if they be free to flow and manifest themselves, that is, if the market be free. Consumers, when given freedom of choice, will not by their purchases, over the long pull, vote against themselves. They will, sooner or later, abandon destructive creativities (harmful goods and services, things in bad taste, and so on) and embrace the crea-

---

[9] Anyone having any question as to how pervasive these interventions are can easily gain an idea by reading *Clichés of Socialism* or my *Anything That's Peaceful,* publications available from the Foundation for Economic Education, Irvington-on-Hudson, New York.

tivities leading to a richer life.[10] Of one other point we can be absolutely certain: In an ideal free market, with government limited to keeping the peace, supply and demand must, of necessity, be in balance; in short, the economy will be sound. No shortages, no surpluses, for each party to every transaction has participated in willing exchange. Each gains. Production, in these circumstances, creates its own purchasing power. The free market and constructive creativities or think-of-thats are economic correlatives.

Now, constrict the market. Let persons who are ignorant of their own ignorance capture positions which put compulsive power at their disposal. Their, not "Thy," will be done! These people will—and do on an enormous scale—coercively take the fruits of the labor of all citizens for the purpose of reconstructing the economy along lines which they (in their ignorance) think best. An economy founded on common consent —the free market—is abandoned in favor of an economy founded on unilateral consent—theirs!

In a free market, we would put men on the moon only if the project were voluntarily underwritten. In an economy presided over by persons who don't know how

---

[10] Noting on every hand consumers making choices so many of us think unwise, some people may regard this claim as invalid. Yet, I submit, no one has ever seen an individual such as I have in mind, which is to say, a person free from the pressures and seductions of state intervention. My claim is a conviction founded on a belief in the evolution of man and evolution's concomitant, freedom. But I must be content with conviction, for there never has been a situation from which proof can be adduced.

little they know, the project is coercively underwritten. You and I have no choice in the matter.

There is no denying the fact that the creativities, think-of-thats, discoveries going into space hardware are fantastic beyond belief. Having billions of dollars —forcibly extorted—at their disposal, our unwise masters swerve creativities into moon machinery, foreign aid, social security, defunct down-towns, distressed areas, slums, and the like, a switch that is not difficult. Scientists, with the capacity to conceive ideas, are easily attracted to this course of action. These people will as readily sell their ingenuity for a coercively collected dollar as for a voluntarily subscribed dollar. A dollar obtained by violence or the threat thereof has the same purchasing power as a dollar obtained in willing exchange.

Of course, some will ask, is the moon project, as well as other governmental activities that go beyond keeping the peace, really destructive? The dire economic consequences do not even need to be understood to know that the answer is affirmative.[11] First, no good end is possible which is achieved by a bad means, for the end pre-exists in the means. This is a principle which we can accept; we do not have to be able to work out the incidence of all means and ends. I take it to be self-evident that any means is bad that rests on coercion of peaceful persons. And, second, if we grasp the point

---

[11] For explanations of the economic consequences, see *Anything That's Peaceful, op. cit.,* chs. I-V.

that these coercive projects stem from ignorance, we ought to suspect that they might be destructive.

What can be the remedy for this dangerous psychosis?[12] Assuredly, it is a compound awareness: the miraculousness of the free market, on the one hand, and what "I" don't know, on the other. At first glance, this suggests going in opposite directions at the same time, but the second glance reveals this to be an illusion. Any growth in awareness, consciousness, perception of whatever field of inquiry is a step in one direction only: toward Truth!

----

[12] Any overassessment of self, for whatever reason, is corrupting and, thus, dangerous—at least to self, if not to others. The axiom, "power corrupts," doubtless can be explained by that overvaluation of self which the possession of power induces. Even that power to influence others which derives from a relative excellence—with its attendant adulation, flattery, applause—makes difficult a balanced judgment of self: the overesteem, unless consciously downgraded, is irresistible; it is so easily believable! But to possess and to exert coercive power over the creative actions of others makes overassessment of self inevitable. The very acceptance of this form of power cancels any ability to apprehend its evil. Acceptance rules out rejection. Thus, not only is the offender corrupted but, as well, all of those beholden to his inflicted ignorance.

· 4 ·

I Don't Know

Any individual who has become aware of the free market and its miraculous performances must realize that
its opposite—socialism—is growing by leaps and
bounds. This growth, at the moment, is not so much in
formal take-over (nationalization of the modes of production) as in political control and the intellectual acceptance of control; socialism, ideologically, is now
American doctrine. This is to say that socialism is not
yet as thoroughly embedded in practice as it is in theory
—but the acceptance of the theory is the preface to inevitable practice. Performance in the world of practical affairs follows on the heels of prevailing ideas.

In any event, socialistic ideas are becoming so popu-
lar that countless "free enterprisers" are either "getting
on the band wagon" or "running for cover." But,
whichever way—one as pitiful as the other—they are
forsaking their role as spokesmen for freedom.

One of the major reasons for this apostasy is clear enough: all too few understand and can make the case for the free market—without which freedom of speech, of the press, of religion are utterly impossible.[1] In the absence of skilled spokesmen, freedom disappears in the U.S.A. as elsewhere.

Making the case for the free market requires a great deal of dedicated homework and learning, among other things, how *not* to give the case away. And unless "I" can everlastingly maintain an awareness of how little "I" know, the chances of becoming an effective expositor of the free market are nil. Here are two tricky and rarely suspected booby traps that victimize many an "I":

1. Attempting to explain how socialism, once installed, can be made to work better than at present.

2. Attempting to explain what would happen to a socialized activity were it de-socialized, leaving the activity to the free market.

I shall try to demonstrate not only that each of these is impossible of realization but that the attempts themselves do the libertarian rationale a distinct disservice.

A FEE Seminar team was invited to Venezuela. We gathered with the participants at a plush hotel sixty miles from Caracas—one of a chain of eleven hostelries

---

[1] See "Freedom Follows the Free Market" by Dean Russell, *The Freeman,* January, 1963.

built, owned, and operated by the national government. The chain has always been deep in the red. A successful businessman (one of our hosts) had once been asked by the government to head this socialized operation. Thinking that socialism might be made to work, *were he in charge,* he accepted the challenge. When he discovered that these hotels required 150 per cent occupancy just to break even, he resigned. Had he known that socialism, by its very nature, can never be made to work, he would have been spared that waste of his energies.

Socialism Defined

Socialism may be defined as the state ownership and control of the *means* of production and exchange and/ or the *results* of production and exchange; but what, really, is it in simple essence? It is a forcible intervention into exchange processes, a power wedge between the willingness of buyers and the willingness of sellers, a coercive interference with what some persons want that other persons are willing to grant. *Socialism, in the final analysis, amounts to the frustration of willing exchange by people who are unaware of how little they know.*

For example: An American desires to exchange his $20 for an Englishman's sweater—nothing involved but a willing swap, no one else's status one whit different after the exchange than before it was made. The

know-it-alls, however, with their police force, insist that
a social interest is involved, that the exchange cannot
be made without a penalty of $5. To the extent that
this transaction is socialized—in this case the penalty
payment of $5—to that degree is the will of two peace-
ful parties frustrated.

How can frustration be made to work? How can
frustration be manipulated into harmony and increased
production? Can any interference with peaceful, willing exchange, regardless of who does the interfering,
do other than wreak havoc?

Many antisocialists, unhappy with the outcome of
socialized activities, feel that these could be improved
were they, rather than other know-it-alls, in charge. So
they seek election or appointment to the government
boards of such activities, under the impression that this
is one way to strike a blow for freedom. This much I
concede: They can, when in charge, *do more of what
they want done* with other people's money than would
be the case were other know-it-alls in charge. But this
is no libertarian accomplishment; it's only a substitu-
tion of one group's know-it-all-ness for another's.

Further, when those of a libertarian bent set out to
make socialism work better, whether by managing the
activity or by their endorsement of legislation which
would modify the socialistic details, they tacitly ap-
prove the socialistic premise and thereby abandon
their own case for the free market. They forswear all
fundamental argument against the socialistic premise

because by their actions they acknowledge that it could be improved were they themselves framing or administering it. "Socialism, were I its manager, wouldn't be so bad." That, I submit, is an emanation from the mind of a know-it-all in words loud and clear.

What am I saying? That a libertarian cannot consistently accept the Postmaster Generalship? Or membership on the municipal power and light board, or whatever? Unless he claims to know how to make socialism work, that is precisely what I am saying.[2] What more effective opposition is there than a polite "No, thank you!" And when asked, "Conceding that TVA is with us, how can it be made to work better than it now does?" what more truthful answer than *"I don't know; I never will know; no one will ever know."* There is no right way to implement a wrong premise!

The student of liberty, if he is not to get off the track, must hope and work for the restoration of the free market and a government restored to its principled role of keeping the peace.[3] Then let him peacefully keep in character by leaving socialistic activities to

---

[2] Even accepting such assignments with a clear mandate to plan their undoing would, I believe, be futile. See "Unscrambling Socialism," *Essays on Liberty,* Volume XII (Irvington-on-Hudson, New York: Foundation for Economic Education, 1965), p. 433.

[3] Inhibiting and penalizing destructive actions such as fraud, violence, misrepresentation, predation—invoking a common justice, keeping the peace—call for a compulsive agency of society: government. The management of destructive activities cannot properly be left to the free market, the nature of which is voluntary and the scope of which is the productive and creative. See my *Government—An Ideal Concept, op. cit.*

those who aren't yet aware of how little they know. Left to their own resources, the bungling of their schemes may become apparent even to themselves and, most certainly, to libertarians who have not fallen into this trap. Why should libertarians absolve the socialists by becoming a party to their unworkable measures?

So much for the first booby trap. But what about its twin, the attempt to explain what would happen were the market freed of state interventionism, that is, were the activities de-socialized?

What Might Have Been?

Skeptics of the free market are forever asking, "Well, how would the free market attend to mail delivery? Education? Or, whatever?" Satisfactorily answer these questions, they imply, or the free market case loses by default. And just as often, aspiring libertarians will stumble into the booby trap; they'll conjure up some sort of an answer.

Now these attempts to answer, regardless of how skilled and ingenious the authors, will have no less than three faults, the least of which is know-it-all-ness. Take the case of mail delivery. A person can no more explain how the free market would attend to mail delivery than his great-grandfather could have explained how television could ever emerge from free market forces!

A more serious fault is that the listening skeptic will conclude that the know-it-all answer is the free market answer and, if that's the best it has to offer, the free market has no valid case. These futile attempts to answer can accomplish no more than to confirm the skeptics in their socialism.

The greatest fault, of course, is that these students of liberty themselves have not yet learned to answer honestly: *"I don't know; I never will know; no one will ever know."* They have not wholly cured themselves of the offending psychosis.

This I-don't-know answer has the virtue of being intelligent, truthful, properly humble, and novel enough to intrigue any skeptic with a searching mind. Conceded, the answer—by itself—sheds no light. But if the skeptic wishes to learn (it is idle to talk to him if he doesn't) and if the aspiring libertarians have observed and can report on how miraculously the free market performs when not politically aborted, skepticism concerning the free market will lessen, faith in what man will accomplish when free to try will increase. In short, light will be shed, education will begin.

How would the free market attend to mail delivery were the postal service de-socialized? *I don't know!* Nor could anyone have known 100 years ago how the free market would develop the means to deliver the human voice from city to city. But take note of these facts: we have maintained mail delivery as a socialized operation; its service is getting worse, not better; its costs and prices are increasing, not decreasing; since 1932 it has accumulated an acknowledged deficit of $10 billion, and the deficits increase annually.[4]

Voice delivery, on the other hand, has been improving. Just a century ago the human voice could be delivered at the speed of sound, but only the distance two people could understand each other's shouting. Today, the human voice is delivered at the speed of light; and as to distance, it's any place on earth—you name it! The service has improved enormously; and the cost has decreased steadily.

In human voice delivery, free market forces have been more or less operative. No one could have predicted in 1865 what form these forces would take during the next hundred years. Even more remarkable, no one can describe how the miracles were performed after the fact. Once we realize that we cannot explain what *has* happened, it becomes obvious that we can never explain what *will* happen.

Nature and Man

The miracles of the market are of a higher and more complex order than the miracles of Nature: What emerges from the free market embraces the miracles of Nature, plus the miracles of human creativity as well. May I repeat, all the artifacts by which we live

---

[4] See "$48,000" by Paul Poirot, *The Freeman*, February, 1965.

are but the application of human creativity to the creativities manifest in Nature.

Reflect on the simpler of these phenomena, the order of Nature. Had you lived on earth before there were any trees, for instance, and been asked, "How can Nature ever make a tree?" you would have answered, "I don't know." Today, were you asked, "How *has* Nature made a tree?" you would be forced to reply, "I don't know." Yet, you can, with considerable certainty, predict that Nature will continue to produce these lovely miracles, *provided conditions favorable to their growth are not aborted.* You can derive from experience, not a how-to-do-it knowledge, but a soundly based faith in the dependability of the biological order.

Such confident expectation is as close as any man can come to knowing how the free market would attend to an activity, were it de-socialized. All about him, in unimaginable profusion, are miracles of the free market, so commonplace that they are taken more for granted than noted and appreciated—like the air we breathe. These, properly apprehended, comprise his experience. But such experience does not give him a how-to-do-it knowledge; it serves only as the basis for a warranted and unshakable faith, a faith in what free men can accomplish—provided conditions favorable to free exchange are not aborted.

The poet who wrote, "Only God can make a tree," was merely acknowledging a common faith. Know-it-alls are never heard trying to refute this; everyone takes it for granted. Yet, if it be asserted that "only God can make a violin"—portions of Nature with human creativity as an added ingredient—the person unaware of how little he knows will have no more hesitancy in subjecting violin production to his masterminding than he has in socializing the airlines, or power and light, or the postal service, or whatever.

Why will people concede that they are unable to mastermind atoms and molecules into the living manifestations of Nature, while at the same time acknowledging no shortcomings at all in themselves when it comes to masterminding something we know far less about: human creativity. *I don't know!*

Gaining a Faith in Freedom

The aspiring libertarian, if he has made the first important step in progress, understands that he does not know how to mastermind the life of a single human being. He concedes that there is an order of Creation over and beyond his own mind, that this order works in diverse and wondrous ways through billions of minds and that he should not in any way abort these miracles. This, however, does not make him a know-nothing. Even though, from his experience, he does not know what will happen, he gains a faith that miracles will happen if creative energies be free to flow.

The accomplished student of liberty acquires a faith that men, when free to try, will perform miracles, a faith extrapolated from experience. But when it comes to predicting the shape of miracles that will show forth from creativity, he takes his place with men, not with clairvoyant demigods. As an aware human being, he must answer, *"I don't know!"*

· 5 ·

Incomprehensible Order

The purpose of this concluding chapter is to throw some light on an important but obscure argument concerning the orderly nature of the free market economy.

Most of us claim an affinity for freedom; but if given a choice between a freedom suspected of chaos and a regimentation assured of order, we would choose the regimentation. We instinctively fear and detest the opposite of order which is chaos, and for a good and compelling reason: man cannot exist unless nearly everything in his life situation is orderly, that is, unless a vast majority of expectations can be taken for granted and counted on to materialize. Man's existence requires a fairly dependable level of order.

For example, man could not exist if he could not count on oxygen in the next volume of air he inhales or if he could not confidently expect Old Sol to rise on the morrow. Were there any doubt about the continual rhythm of these events, the doubt alone would do him in. Or let only minor mishaps intrude themselves into the autonomic nervous system, which beyond conscious effort, controls heartbeats, breathing, peristalsis, glandular and countless other bodily activities, and man's earthly days are over. Man is a nervous animal, and one of the conditions of survival is a dependable, orderly sequence of things to come.

Nor need we limit our observations to the necessity for orderliness in nature or in man's person; also required is an orderly social environment so that man can know what to expect, within limits, from his fellow men. Suppose, for instance, that no one could be counted on to keep his word, that promises were meaningless, that capriciousness in everything were the rule: buy a can of beans only to find it filled with mud; hire workers who refuse to work; contract at one price and get charged a higher price; earn a livelihood that is subject to confiscation at anyone else's pleasure; act peacefully but with no security of body and limb; and so on and on. Man can endure but little of this; he can't cope with life at sixes and sevens, with many things in the realm of uncertainty. And because of this he will pay almost any price—even his freedom—for certainty, for order. Indeed, when confronted with but a modicum of chaos, he will accept with alacrity numerous variations of the goose step, those constraints which appear to minimize uncertainties and thus give him the semblance of order.

Most of these "goose steps" which appear as a relief from chaos such as controls of prices, wages, rents, hours of labor, or "planned" production and exchange —economic freezes, one might say—are, in fact, contrary to order. These rigidities are necessarily interferences with men's choices and result in chaos.

Millions of Private Decisions

The truth is that order and chaos in the economic realm are the reverse of what is generally supposed to be the case. It is doubtful if anyone could more strikingly phrase this common confusion than was done by one of our country's most powerful labor officials. He wrote:

Only a moron would believe that the millions of private economic decisions being made independently of each other will somehow harmonize in the end and bring us out where we want to be.[1]

It's one thing to confess to not knowing much; it is quite another matter to be referred to as a moron for believing that the free market can gratify our goals, that is, "bring us out where we want to be."

If "where we want to be" is under the dictatorial thumb of know-it-alls, this statement might make sense. Otherwise, it evidences an utter confusion as to the

---

[1] See *The New York Times,* June 30, 1962.

nature of man, of personal evolution, and of the free market.

Analogous to the labor official's "millions of private economic decisions" are the creative decisions within each human being, such as: an octillion atoms in an incomprehensible array of configurations; some 30 trillion cells; bone marrow producing one billion red blood cells every 60 seconds; each kidney having some 5 million complex glomeruli; a diencephalon, a portion of the brain stem that acts independently of consciousness; a cranium filled with nerve tissues having a seemingly unlimited supply of neuroblasts—unfinished nerve cells—which can, with conscious effort and other disciplines, be transformed into functioning neurons. Such enormous, utterly staggering phenomena of man's composition—"fearfully and wonderfully made," as he is—cannot be grasped as other than chaos by a finite mind. These trillions upon trillions of data, in each human being, about which we have but the dimmest notions, can easily tempt one to conclude: "Only a moron would believe that these will somehow harmonize in the end and bring us out where we want to be."

Were these data chaotic, as they appear to be, we would then have to admit that order is actually born of disorder, for they do harmonize in the end and bring us out where we want to be: a human being, the most amazing example of order within our awareness. Why not simply confess that these data are an order of Creation which we do not comprehend? That we are unable to bring their order within our narrow purview?

The complex of creativities flowing through the minds of men over the millennia, the "chaos" which caused the labor official to refer to them as "millions of economic decisions made independently of each other," proceed from the same Source as the complex data observed in each human being. If not aborted they, like the complexities in man, result in order. True, we do not seriously question the point as it relates to man; we are so dumbfounded by the mystery of life that we readily concede that only God can make a tree—or a man. But there is all too little of this faith and humility as it concerns the free market. In the latter, as we witness millions of economic decisions made independently of each other, we will, if not perceptive, refer to them as chaotic; whereas, in fact, we are viewing an order the complexity of which cannot be brought within our limited grasp of things. What we lightly pass over as chaos is but a reflection of our failure to comprehend.

Take only a casual look at our economic world. Visit Russia, Red China, Cuba, East Germany. Like our labor official and many of our educators and business "leaders," these unfortunate people do not understand how millions of economic decisions made independently of each other could possibly harmonize in the end and bring about efficacious results; that is, their minds, deficient in awareness, sensing only chaos in the complex data of the free and unfettered market, proceed to bring "order" out of it. How? A Mr. Big takes over and substitutes his one-source decisions for the millions of decisions that would otherwise be made independently of each other. But observe that one man's orders, aimed at bringing about his singular idea of order, result in everyone else's chaos, as deadening in the end as if he himself were to take over the forces that make him a human being. He can no more master-mind market data than he can the data of his own being. The consequences would be as disastrous in the one case as in the other.

Getting Used to the Chains

Unfortunately, the chaos brought on by one-source decisions—the practice of political know-it-all-ness—is seldom thought of as chaos once the subjects have endured the oppression of their own spirits for a short time. Like wild animals placed in zoos, or human beings in slavery, or criminals in prison—as soon as the shock of contrast is over they come to think of their fetters as more a part of ordered than chaotic life.

But let an American housewife, for instance, accustomed as she is to an economy in which millions of decisions are made more or less independently of each other—where the free market is somewhat approximated—awaken on the morrow to a Russian one-source decision situation: the larder bare, no telephone, no car, no taxi available, standing in line hours on end only to find a scrap of this or that for her family; freedom of expression, of writing, of religion denied; a suppression of desires, aspirations, ambitions. What a shock such a sudden contrast would evoke! Mrs. America would, indeed, be conscious of an unbelievable chaos; she would correctly conclude that a great deal of order had been removed from her life situation.

The more a country's economy is politically ordered or "planned," the more chaotic is production and exchange. Conversely, the freer the market—the greater the extent that economic decisions are made independently of each other—the more order there is in production and exchange.

Try making purchases in Havana and then try in Chicago or Keokuk. You will have little doubt as to where the order is. Or, if it be argued that Cuba hasn't had time to "make socialism work," then compare experiences in Moscow with Hong Kong. Russia has been at it for nearly half a century! Also bear in mind that the chaos which is manifest in the Moscow market place has its origin in a one-source-decision apparatus; that the order which is manifest in the Hong Kong market place has its origin in millions of economic decisions made independently of each other.

Order is not necessarily characterized by systems in a static, motionless relationship, as is so often thought. Take, for instance, heavenly bodies: *motion in relation to one another is of their nature;* they manifest order only when orbiting. Were they to behave contrary to their nature, that is, were their swift flight through the void to halt, cosmic chaos would result.

Now, reflect on neat rows of cemetery headstones. As distinguished from heavenly bodies, *a static, motionless relationship of each to the others is of their nature*. Were these headstones to go into motion or orbit, a behavior contrary to their nature, we would observe the contrary of order: chaos!

These observations are meant to suggest that it is the frustration of the nature of a system that spells chaos—order consisting of what is in harmony with a system's nature. What is order in one instance might be chaos in another. The nature of the system prescribes the characteristics of the order and the chaos peculiar to it.

Man's Nature Is to Emerge

Consider the nature of man. The Greek philosopher, Heraclitus, amusingly oversimplified it when he suggested that man is on earth as in an egg; that he cannot go on forever being a good egg; that he has to hatch or rot. Man's nature, as distinguished from that of other animals, is to evolve, to emerge; it is to grow in consciousness, awareness, perception; it is to make strides as a rational animal and, eventually, to make choices with intelligent discrimination and, to some extent, to will his own actions. Man—potentially, at

least—must be included in creative phenomena and
any thwarting or frustration of this, his sensitive and
spiritual nature, must induce chaos. The man-imposed
goose step in its social, political, and economic ver-
sions—the headstone kind of static, motionless order—
is the antithesis of any order that has to do with ex-
panding consciousness.

Man, in the light of his destiny, is not a static organ-
ism. This is unthinkable. Furthermore, the free and
unfettered market is but the unfrustrated economic
manifestation of man's creative, emerging, spiritual
dynamism. Man enjoys freedom only if he be free to
make decisions and act on the basis of his choices. This
is self-evident; it needs no proof. Thus, it follows that
man can be free only if his peaceful, creative actions
are not aborted. This is to say that man can be free to
emerge in the direction of his destiny only if his market
—economic expressions of men—be free. The free
market, founded on economic decisions made independently of each other, resting, as it does, on common
consent, is consonant and in harmony with freely act-
ing man. Dynamism, in this context—moving, flowing,
creative, kinetic energy—is as much a characteristic
of the free market as it is of the individual human being, man and his market being but two parts of a
whole; this dynamism is of the nature of each. Order
in either case—man or his market—exists only as this
dynamism, showing forth peacefully and creatively,
finds unfrustrated expression. Any man-imposed goose

step must breed chaos just as surely as if some political know-it-all were to stop the heavenly bodies in their orbits.

I have tried to suggest that we must look to the nature of a system to determine what is order and what is chaos. Whenever we impose the headstone variety of static, motionless order to man and his market, that is, whenever we substitute one-source decisions for millions of decisions made independently of each other, we get chaos for our unintelligent pains. And it is axiomatic that freedom must disappear as we practice the error!

To illustrate the mysterious order of the free market, think of any one of a million goods or services: corn flakes, atomizers, hats, automobiles, radios, TV sets, telephones, machine tools, computers, illumination, and so on, things that are left more or less to countless decisions made independently of each other. Millions upon millions of tiny think-of-thats, little creativities, individual acceptances and rejections, whims, likes and dislikes—forces too numerous ever to recount and which appear as chaos but are, instead, incomprehensible order—miraculously combine to form the fantastic order of these artifacts by which we live. Observe that the order of these is so perfect, their production and exchange and their demand and supply so nicely balanced, that we take them as much for granted as we do our next heart beat. Rarely a second thought! No argument! Further, the very fact that an automobile, for instance, is an orderly mechanism is testimony in itself that it originated out of incomprehensible order, not out of chaos.

Now reflect on those goods and services no longer entrusted to the millions of economic decisions made independently of each other in a free market, but delegated instead to one-source governmental decisions as a way of bringing "order out of chaos." To cite a few: an ever-enlarging part of employment, many wages, prices, exchanges; a good deal of housing; wheat, tobacco, corn, cotton; more and more power and light; education, money value, and others. Observe the imbalances and note that these are the only goods and services we ever argue about. By this method, we do not bring order out of chaos but, rather, chaos out of incomprehensible order! The very fact that these goods and services are now in a chaotic state is testimony in itself that incomprehensible order has been converted to chaos.

Barriers to Trade, and Growth

One consequence of confusing order and chaos is a static market and its aftermath, a frustration of man's nature, the free market being but the extension or manifestation of free men. Damage cannot be done to the free market without an equal damage to man's nature. When men are compelled to look to a one-source decision instead of to the individual decisions of men, man is robbed of his wholeness. Self-responsibility, the corollary of self-decision, and the wellspring of man's growth, gives way to cheap politics, mass plunder, pressure grouping, protectionism. Any time a society is organized in such a manner that a premium is put on the obeisance paid to political know-it-alls and when little, if any, reward attends integrity and self-reliance, the members of that society will tend more to rot than to hatch!

If human beings were meant to be ordered in the manner of cemetery headstones, is it conceivable that any one man or organized group of men would be capable of planning and directing the lives and activities of all the others? If all men possessed only the similarities and potentialities of headstones, which of the headstones are capable of directing the others?

It is precisely because we differ from one another, because—as even the communists admit—each has his needs, that human beings require freedom to express those needs and to satisfy them, individual by individual. The free market is an agency for the expression and sorting of these countless differences: in the bidding and asking prices, the voluntary buying and selling of scarce resources, whereby each may pursue his own proper interests without infringing upon or denying the nature and the interests of any other peaceful person. When alternatives have been sought and applied to the open market, the result always has been some variation of the master-slave arrangement, with one man's order bringing chaos into the lives of others.

We are led to speculate on why this confusion about order and chaos. While there are few who put the case for the headstone variety of order as boldly and as honestly as the labor official, all who argue for and introduce rigidities into the market are up to the same mischief. Sadly, not a category of the population is exempt: teachers share heavily in the error as do preachers, business and civic leaders; indeed, were it said, "Let him who is without sin cast the first stone," few rocks would fly.

Torn in Two Directions

When the error is as general as this one, the cause must lie very deep. Inspect this suspicion of mine and see if it makes sense: Man—with notable exceptions—suffers a fearful contradiction. There is on the one hand his God-given nature (1) to be born on this earth, (2) to grow and to emerge in consciousness, and (3) to age and, eventually, to depart this earth. This cosmic, evolutionary tug is a powerful force but not as a rule, a force about which man is sharply conscious.

On the other hand, there is man's slight, budding ability to reason and choose—an ability still linked to an abysmal ignorance. Being but dimly aware of his natural destiny and of how little he knows, man tends to ascribe to his reason an omniscience out of all proportion to what the facts warrant. Thus, human beings are confronted with two powerful commandments that are in conflict, one might say, two tugs in opposite directions.

Man's nature calls for a flexing, an improving use and a continuing growth of the faculties, regardless of how uncomfortable or painful this perpetual stretching may be. In opposition, is his defective ability to reason which commands him to remove himself from the struggle, to get out of rather than into life, in a word, to seek ease.

That man's embryonic ability to reason is often a more powerful tug than is his natural destiny is evidenced by his fear of earthly departure. Viewed rationally, it would seem that departing this earth is as congenial to man's nature as being born.[2] Both arrival and departure are but two parts of life's equation; whatever has a beginning has a conclusion. Yet, note how general the fear is.

Afraid to Die—or Live

But now to my point: Not only is man—most men —fearful of that aspect of his nature which is his earthly demise, but he is equally fearful of that aspect of his nature which is life's living! Observe the tendency

---

[2] ". . . from an evolutive point of view the greatest invention of Nature is death." See *Human Destiny, op. cit.,* ch. V.

to run away from problems, obstacles; the passion for wealth as a means of relief from employment; the yearning for security; the ambition to retire; and, specifically to my point, the dread of competition. As a consequence of this defective reasoning, man generally seeks a static, motionless kind of order—the headstone variety—while his nature calls for an order of the dynamic variety which, unless he is highly perceptive, he looks upon as chaos.

Competition—our attitude toward it—gets to the heart of the problem. It is a powerful antistatic force, the enemy of status; competition is the activating agent, the gyrator, so to speak, in man's life and in his market; it keeps things whipped up, moving, changing, improving, always uncomfortable, sometimes painful, but, nonetheless, dynamic. A noncompetitive society is a monopolistic society. Competition is the ally of man's natural destiny and, thus, it is the preservative of his freedom; without competition man's market and man himself would fall into a state of lethargy; the static kind of order would prevail, in which freedom is impossible.

Be it noted that human beings, as if in response to their natural and evolutionary destiny, favor competition for everyone—except one person: self! As for self, excuses take command and seek protection against the uneasiness competition imposes.

When everyone favors competition for me—except me—it would seem that competition has it, that protection for me would be impossible. But when we let know-it-alls with a constabulary intervene in the market place, that is, in creative human actions, thus giving to government a power sway not sanctioned by sound principle, we render competition ineffective and, thus, poke a dangerous hole in the armor of freedom. It is called logrolling: "I'll vote for your protection if you'll vote for mine." Of course, as protectionism spreads, competition correspondingly decreases, monopoly increases, and freedom diminishes. We achieve the headstone kind of order which, for man, is chaos.

We may never be able to mend the aforementioned flaw until we acquire a more rational view of competition—human dynamics—than we now have; not a more rational view of competition for others—this we possess—but for self. If I concede that competition is desirable for all others, how, rationally and logically, can I make an exception of myself? It doesn't make sense.

Keeping in mind man's natural, evolutionary destiny, competition is as good for me as for anyone else. Admittedly, experience helps in being rational: about forty years ago my competitors ran me out of the wholesale produce business. I had to sell my home, furniture, car, everything to pay the creditors. Broke! A painful experience, indeed! But had it not been for competition, I would, no doubt, be in that business today. Not that there is anything wrong with being a wholesale produce merchant; it is that I did not belong in that role. Others were better fitted for it. And, important to me, I was led—not happily at first—to discover that there were other employments that better suited my aptitudes. Competition made it possible for me to discover how best to allocate those few resources peculiar to my own person. Competition is at once the economizer and activator; it helps to keep us on the creative move and to find the niche appropriate to the distinctive abilities of each.

Let Freedom Reign!

If the foregoing reflections are valid, it is certain that freedom in the market, without which other freedoms are impossible, can exist only as creativities of the peaceful variety remain unrestrained. True, this calls for an order so complex that it gives the appearance of chaos; yet, it is order, however incomprehensible. This is the order observed in a living tree, in emerging man, in Creation going on before our eyes.

When we mistake incomprehensible order for chaos we leave ourselves open to the more or less innocent deceptions of the know-it-alls. These people, when they succeed in acquiring coercive power, impose restraints on the free flowing of creative energy. Yet, the free market works many of its wonders in spite of their meddling. Unaware of how little they know, they are led to believe that it is their restraints which account for the wonders; and because of this erroneous correlation, they claim credit for the accomplishments which take place despite their subversions. This is bad enough in itself, but it is fatal if we believe their claims. For, if we do, we shall substitute their know-it-all-ness for the miraculous market; we shall look to them for our blessings and not to Creation—a fearful penalty for a needless naivete. Little else than a sharpened awareness is required to avoid the deceptions by those who know not that they know so little.

May our awareness never dim to the point that we shall rewrite our verse to read:

> Poems are made by gods like me,
> Thus only man can make a tree.